CHICKEN BASED DOG FOOD COOKBOOK

Dr. Doris Meany

Disclaimer:

The content within this book is offered solely for general information purposes. The author and publisher disclaim any responsibility for actions taken in reliance on the material herein. Although every endeavor has been made to ensure the accuracy and comprehensiveness of the information, the author and publisher do not provide any explicit or implied guarantees regarding the reliability, appropriateness, or accessibility of the content contained in this book.

OTHER BOOKS BY THE AUTHOR

High Protein Dog Food Cookbook

Grain-free Dog Food Cookbook

Slow Cooker Dog Food Cookbook

IF YOU WOULD LIKE TO CHECK OUT MORE BOOKS BY DR.DORIS MEANY, SCAN THE QR CODE BELOW

TABLE OF CONTENTS

CHICKEN BASED DOG FOOD COOKBOOK

INTRODUCTION

In a world brimming with uncertainties and rapid change, there exists one steadfast certainty that has withstood the test of time: our profound and unwavering love for our canine companions. These four-legged friends, with their unwavering loyalty, boundless joy, and endless capacity for love, weave themselves into the very fabric of our lives. As a devoted dog lover and a seasoned veteran in the field of veterinary nutrition for over two decades, I found myself deeply entrenched in a world dominated by commercial pet food—bags of kibble, rows of canned meals, and shelves lined with treats, each promising the pinnacle of health and nutrition for our beloved furry friends.

However, amidst this sea of choices, doubts began to sow seeds of uncertainty within me. The prices of these commercial offerings soared to new heights, leaving me disconcerted about their true value and quality. But it was a singular, heart-stopping moment that served as a clarion call, an experience that shook me to my core and upended my trust in the very products I had spent years advocating. A seemingly innocuous dog treat, purchased with the intention of delighting my faithful companion, nearly became a tragic end to a story of love and companionship. That jarring incident served as a catalyst, prompting me to reassess the trajectory of our canine companions' nutrition.

CHICKEN BASED DOG FOOD COOKBOOK

Faced with the soaring costs and dubious quality of store-bought pet food, I stood at a crossroads—a pivotal juncture that demanded a decision. It was a choice between continuing down the uncertain path of commercial dog food, fraught with hidden dangers, or seizing the reins and taking matters into my own hands.

Driven by a potent cocktail of love for dogs and a wealth of expertise acquired over years of veterinary practice, I embarked on a journey that would reshape not just my own life but the lives of countless dogs and their devoted owners. I made a solemn vow to create a solution that would seamlessly merge the precision of a seasoned veterinary dietician with the unwavering dedication of a pet parent. Thus began my foray into the realm of homemade dog food—a world teeming with possibilities and potential.

My kitchen became a laboratory, a place where innovation danced with culinary finesse and scientific rigor. Armed with an arsenal of ingredients, cooking utensils, and an insatiable thirst for perfection, I ventured into uncharted territory. Countless trials and myriad experiments became my daily routine, each culinary creation bearing the stamp of meticulous care and unwavering attention to detail.

In this grand pursuit of crafting nutritionally sound meals and delectable treats for our canine companions, the idea of chicken-based recipes emerged as a beacon of promise. The sizzle of chicken on a skillet became a symphony of flavors waiting to be orchestrated, each ingredient carefully selected to meet not just taste bud satisfaction but also the specific nutritional needs of our furry friends.

Weeks stretched into months as I toiled tirelessly, refining recipes that were not just nourishing but were crafted with the utmost care and expertise. It was a labor of love—a quest to ensure that every dog that dined on these homemade meals and treats would not just survive but thrive.

As I began sharing these meticulously curated recipes with my clientele—those who placed their trust not just in my expertise but in my unyielding commitment to their pets' well-being—the response was nothing short of extraordinary. Word spread organically, fueled not by marketing strategies but by the resounding testimonials of happy, healthy dogs and grateful owners. Referrals cascaded in, each one a testament to the transformative power of homemade, chicken-based dog food.

Amidst the chorus of praise and the palpable impact on the lives of these dogs, an idea began to take root—an idea that transcended the boundaries of my clinic or immediate circle. I envisioned a world where every dog owner, regardless of their geographical location or financial constraints, could access these life-changing recipes. It was this seedling of an idea that blossomed into the book you hold in your hands today.

This cookbook is not merely a compendium of recipes; it's a chronicle of passion, dedication, and an unyielding love for our furry companions. It's a culmination of trials, errors, and triumphs—a labor of love meticulously curated with the hope of transforming the lives of dogs and their devoted humans across the globe.

Within these pages lie not just delicious recipes but a comprehensive guide brimming with insights and tips garnered from years of unwavering dedication. It's a testament to the unwavering belief that every dog deserves the best—a bowl filled not just with nourishment but with love, care, and a dash of culinary delight.

So, to all the dog lovers out there, weary of the uncertainty shrouding commercial pet food, to those who yearn for a deeper connection with their pets through homemade goodness, this book is your beacon of hope. It's a promise—a promise of healthier, happier, tail-wagging days ahead, shared with your beloved furry companions.

Together, let us embark on this culinary adventure guided by love, fueled by the unwavering bond we share with our dogs. Welcome to a world where chicken reigns supreme, where every meal is a celebration of love, health, and the joy of being a dog parent. Embrace this journey with open hearts and eager hands as we unravel the secrets to creating meals that nourish not just their bodies but also their souls.

CHAPTER 1

HEALTH BENEFITS OF CHICKEN-BASED DIETS FOR DOGS

Your dog's health is paramount, and what better way to ensure their well-being than through a carefully crafted diet? As you embark on understanding the significance of chicken-based diets for your furry companion, you'll uncover a wealth of benefits that contribute to their overall health and vitality. In this chapter, we'll delve deep into the protein power of chicken, explore the essential nutrients it offers, and discover how it can help manage allergies in your beloved canine friend.

PROTEIN POWER: CHICKEN AS A PRIMARY INGREDIENT

Protein serves as the building block for your dog's body, supporting muscle development, tissue repair, and overall growth. When it comes to protein sources in dog food, few options rival the nutritional potency of chicken. As a primary ingredient, chicken provides a high-quality, easily digestible protein that is crucial for your dog's well-being.

One of the key advantages of chicken protein lies in its amino acid profile. Amino acids are the fundamental components of protein, and chicken offers a balanced array of these essential nutrients. These amino acids aid in the synthesis of enzymes, hormones, and antibodies, bolstering your dog's immune system and supporting various physiological functions.

Moreover, chicken protein is highly bioavailable, meaning it can be efficiently absorbed and utilized by your dog's body. This efficient utilization ensures that your dog receives the maximum benefit from the protein they consume, promoting optimal health and vitality.

Chicken-based diets also tend to be more palatable for dogs, enticing even the pickiest eaters. This high palatability not only makes mealtime enjoyable for your furry friend but also encourages adequate consumption, ensuring they receive the necessary nutrients for their well-being.

ESSENTIAL NUTRIENTS IN CHICKEN FOR CANINE HEALTH

Beyond its protein content, chicken is a rich source of essential nutrients vital for your dog's health. These nutrients include but are not limited to:

Vitamins: Chicken contains various vitamins such as B vitamins (B6, B12, niacin), which play crucial roles in energy metabolism, nervous system function, and cell health. Additionally, vitamins like A and D contribute to vision, skin health, and calcium absorption.

Minerals: Chicken provides minerals like phosphorus and selenium, essential for bone health, muscle function, and antioxidant support. These minerals contribute to overall vitality and well-being in your dog.

Fatty Acids: Omega-3 and Omega-6 fatty acids present in chicken promote healthy skin and coat, reduce inflammation, and support cardiovascular health. These fatty acids are essential for your dog's overall wellness.

The combination of these nutrients in chicken creates a holistic approach to your dog's nutritional needs, ensuring they receive a balanced diet that supports their growth, energy levels, and immune system.

MANAGING ALLERGIES WITH CHICKEN

Contrary to popular belief, chicken can serve as a beneficial ingredient in managing canine allergies. While some dogs may have sensitivities or allergies to certain proteins, chicken often emerges as a hypoallergenic option.

In many cases, food allergies in dogs stem from ingredients such as beef or grains. Chicken, with its relatively low allergenic potential, can be a suitable alternative for dogs with sensitive stomachs or allergies to other common protein sources. Its digestibility and mild nature make it a valuable choice for formulating hypoallergenic diets.

Embracing a chicken-based diet for your canine companion offers a myriad of health benefits. From its exceptional protein content and abundance of essential nutrients to its potential in managing allergies, chicken stands as a versatile and nutritious ingredient in your dog's diet. By prioritizing their health through a thoughtfully crafted diet, you can contribute significantly to your dog's longevity, energy levels, and overall well-being.

NOTE FROM THE AUTHOR!

Hello, before we dive into the next chapter, I want to extend my heartfelt gratitude to you for joining me on this remarkable journey. Exploring the realm of homemade dog food and nutrition can spark curiosity and raise questions. As a fellow dog lover, I'm here to be your guiding light.

Your decision to invest in this book means everything to me. I'm dedicated to supporting you at every turn. Whether you seek clarity, guidance, or a deeper understanding, don't hesitate to reach out via email at: **drdorismeanyvet@gmail.com**

I promise to personally respond within 24 hours, eager to assist as you strive for improved wellness. Your feedback and questions are immensely valuable. I genuinely appreciate the privilege of accompanying you through this journey.

CHAPTER 2
CHICKEN AS A NUTRITIOUS BASE

In the realm of crafting wholesome, nutritious meals for your canine companion, chicken stands out as a versatile and nourishing foundation. This chapter will delve into the nuances of utilizing chicken as the primary ingredient in your dog's diet. From choosing the right cuts to handling and preparing chicken for optimal nutrition, and even tailoring chicken-based diets for different dog breeds, this comprehensive chapter will empower you to create delectable and healthful meals for your furry friend.

CHOOSING THE RIGHT CUTS OF CHICKEN

Selecting the appropriate cuts of chicken is crucial in ensuring your dog receives the maximum nutritional benefits. When it comes to choosing chicken for your dog's diet, consider the following factors:

Lean Cuts: Opt for lean cuts of chicken, such as boneless, skinless breasts or thighs. These cuts contain high-quality protein without excessive fat content, promoting muscle health and overall well-being in your dog.

Avoid Bones: While bones may seem natural, they can pose choking hazards or lead to digestive issues. Remove bones entirely from chicken cuts before incorporating them into your dog's meals.

Organic and Free-Range Options: If possible, choose organic or free-range chicken. These options tend to have fewer additives, hormones, or antibiotics, offering a cleaner and more natural protein source for your dog.

Cooked vs. Raw: Some dog owners prefer feeding raw diets, while others opt for cooked chicken. If you choose to feed raw chicken, ensure it is of the highest quality and sourced from reputable suppliers. If cooking, avoid using excessive seasoning or additives that may be harmful to your dog.

HANDLING AND PREPARING CHICKEN FOR DOGS

Proper handling and preparation of chicken are paramount to prevent contamination and ensure your dog's safety. Follow these guidelines when handling and preparing chicken for your furry friend:

Storage and Thawing: Store chicken in the refrigerator or freezer to prevent spoilage. Thaw frozen chicken in the refrigerator overnight or under cold running water to maintain freshness.

Sanitary Precautions: Practice good hygiene by thoroughly washing your hands, utensils, and surfaces that come into contact with raw chicken to prevent cross-contamination.

Cooking Methods: When cooking chicken for your dog, avoid using excessive oil, seasonings, or spices that may upset their stomach. Consider boiling, baking, or grilling chicken without adding potentially harmful ingredients.

Portion Control: Properly portion the chicken according to your dog's size, age, and dietary requirements. Avoid overfeeding to prevent digestive issues and obesity.

CHICKEN-BASED DIET FOR DIFFERENT DOG BREEDS

Different dog breeds have varying nutritional needs and dietary requirements. While chicken serves as an excellent base for most dogs, tailoring the diet to suit specific breeds can optimize their health and well-being. Consider the following breed-specific guidelines:

Small Breeds: Smaller breeds may benefit from smaller, bite-sized portions of chicken. They often have higher metabolisms, so dividing their meals into smaller, more frequent servings may be advantageous.

Large Breeds: Larger breeds may require larger portions of chicken to meet their energy needs. However, be cautious of overfeeding, as excessive weight can strain their joints and lead to health issues.

Active Breeds: Dogs with high activity levels, such as working or sporting breeds, may benefit from additional protein and calorie intake. Chicken provides a protein-rich source to support their active lifestyle.

Senior or Less Active Dogs: Older or less active dogs may require reduced portions of chicken to prevent weight gain. Consider incorporating other ingredients like vegetables or grains to provide balanced nutrition while managing calorie intake.

Chicken serves as an exceptional and versatile foundation for crafting nutritious meals for your beloved canine companion. By understanding how to choose the right cuts, handle and prepare chicken safely, and tailor diets for different breeds, you can ensure that your dog receives a balanced and wholesome diet that supports their health and vitality.

Remember, while chicken is an excellent source of protein and nutrients, it should be part of a well-rounded diet that incorporates other essential ingredients to meet all of your dog's nutritional needs.

CHAPTER 3
RECIPES FOR BALANCED CHICKEN-BASED MEALS

1) CLUCK 'N' QUINOA DELIGHT

Cook Time: 25 minutes

Servings: 4

Ingredients:

- 2 cups cooked chicken, shredded
- 1 cup quinoa, cooked
- 1 cup carrots, finely chopped
- 1/2 cup green beans, chopped

Instructions:

1) Mix shredded chicken, cooked quinoa, carrots, and green beans in a bowl.
2) Serve in portions suitable for your dog's size.

Nutritional Info: Protein: 20g, Fat: 8g, Carbs: 15g

Tips: Add a drizzle of olive oil for an extra boost of healthy fats.

2) POULTRY POWER BOWL

Cook Time: 30 minutes

Servings: 3

Ingredients:

- 1 1/2 cups chicken breast, diced
- 1 sweet potato, cubed
- 1 cup broccoli florets
- 1 tablespoon coconut oil

Instructions:

1) Cook chicken in a pan with coconut oil until lightly browned.

2) Steam sweet potato and broccoli until tender.

3) Combine all ingredients and serve.

Nutritional Info: Protein: 18g, Fat: 5g, Carbs: 20g

Tips: Use lean cuts of chicken for lower fat content.

3) Chicken & Veggie Stir-Fry

Cook Time: 20 minutes

Servings: 4

Ingredients:

- 2 cups cooked chicken, sliced
- 1 cup bell peppers, sliced
- 1 cup snow peas
- 2 tablespoons low-sodium soy sauce

Instructions:

1) Stir-fry chicken in a pan until cooked through.

2) Add sliced peppers and snow peas, cook until veggies are tender.

3) Stir in soy sauce and serve.

Nutritional Info: Protein: 22g, Fat: 6g, Carbs: 12g

Tips: Ensure the soy sauce is low in sodium to avoid excessive salt intake.

4) CHICKEN BERRY CRUNCH

Cook Time: 15 minutes

Servings: 2

Ingredients:

- 1 cup cooked chicken, diced
- 1/2 cup blueberries
- 1/2 cup strawberries, chopped
- 1/4 cup pumpkin puree

Instructions:

1) Mix diced chicken, blueberries, strawberries, and pumpkin puree in a bowl.
2) Serve in portions appropriate for your dog's size.

Nutritional Info: Protein: 12g, Fat: 4g, Carbs: 10g

Tips: Use fresh, unsweetened berries for maximum nutrients.

5) CHICKEN & RICE MEDLEY

Cook Time: 30 minutes

Servings: 4

Ingredients:

- 2 cups cooked chicken, shredded
- 1 cup brown rice, cooked
- 1/2 cup peas
- 1/2 cup carrots, diced

Instructions:

1) Mix shredded chicken, cooked rice, peas, and diced carrots in a bowl.
2) Portion and serve when cooled.

Nutritional Info: Protein: 18g, Fat: 6g, Carbs: 20g

Tips: Use brown rice for added fiber and nutrients.

6) CHEESY CHICKEN SURPRISE

Cook Time: 25 minutes

Servings: 3

Ingredients:

- 1 1/2 cups cooked chicken, chopped
- 1/2 cup cottage cheese
- 1/4 cup spinach, chopped
- 1 tablespoon olive oil

Instructions:

1) Mix chicken, cottage cheese, and chopped spinach in a bowl.
2) Drizzle with olive oil and serve.

Nutritional Info: Protein: 16g, Fat: 7g, Carbs: 5g

Tips: Use low-fat cottage cheese for a lighter option.

7) CHICKEN & PUMPKIN STEW

Cook Time: 40 minutes

Servings: 5

Ingredients:

- 2 cups cooked chicken, cubed
- 1 cup pumpkin, diced
- 1/2 cup green beans, chopped
- 1 cup low-sodium chicken broth

Instructions:

1) Combine chicken, diced pumpkin, green beans, and chicken broth in a pot.

2) Simmer until vegetables are tender, then cool before serving.

Nutritional Info: Protein: 20g, Fat: 6g, Carbs: 10g

Tips: Use fresh pumpkin or unsweetened canned pumpkin puree.

8) CHICKEN & LENTIL FEAST

Cook Time: 35 minutes

Servings: 4

Ingredients:

- 1 1/2 cups cooked chicken, shredded
- 1 cup cooked lentils
- 1/2 cup carrots, grated
- 1/4 cup parsley, chopped

Instructions:

1) Mix shredded chicken, cooked lentils, grated carrots, and chopped parsley in a bowl.
2) Serve once cooled.

Nutritional Info: Protein: 17g, Fat: 5g, Carbs: 18g

Tips: Use green or brown lentils for added fiber.

9) CHICKEN & FISH COMBO

Cook Time: 20 minutes

Servings: 3

Ingredients:

- 1 cup cooked chicken, diced
- 1/2 cup cooked fish (like salmon or cod), flaked
- 1/4 cup carrots, finely chopped
- 1 tablespoon coconut oil

Instructions:

1) Mix diced chicken, flaked fish, chopped carrots, and coconut oil in a bowl.
2) Serve in suitable portions.

Nutritional Info: Protein: 18g, Fat: 8g, Carbs: 5g

Tips: Ensure the fish is deboned and free from seasoning or added ingredients.

10) CHICKEN & EGG SCRAMBLE

Cook Time: 15 minutes

Servings: 2

Ingredients:

- 1 cup cooked chicken, shredded
- 2 eggs
- 1/2 cup spinach, chopped
- 1 tablespoon olive oil

Instructions:

1) Heat olive oil in a pan, add eggs and scramble.
2) Add shredded chicken and chopped spinach, cook until heated through.
3) Serve when cooled.

Nutritional Info: Protein: 15g, Fat: 10g, Carbs: 3g

Tips: Use free-range eggs for added nutrients.

11) CHICKEN LIVER DELIGHT

Cook Time: 25 minutes

Servings: 4

Ingredients:

- 1 1/2 cups chicken liver, cooked and diced
- 1/2 cup sweet potato, mashed
- 1/4 cup green peas
- 1 tablespoon coconut oil

Instructions:

1) Mix diced chicken liver, mashed sweet potato, green peas, and coconut oil.
2) Portion and serve when cooled.

Nutritional Info: Protein: 20g, Fat: 9g, Carbs: 12g

Tips: Ensure the chicken liver is fully cooked to avoid any health risks.

12)　CHICKEN & CHICKPEA STEW

Cook Time: 35 minutes

Servings: 4

Ingredients:

- 2 cups cooked chicken, shredded
- 1 cup cooked chickpeas
- 1/2 cup carrots, diced
- 1/4 cup parsley, chopped

Instructions:

1) Combine shredded chicken, cooked chickpeas, diced carrots, and chopped parsley in a pot.
2) Simmer until carrots are tender, then serve.

Nutritional Info: Protein: 18g, Fat: 6g, Carbs: 20g

Tips: Mash some chickpeas for smaller dogs to ease digestion.

13) CHICKEN & OAT MEATBALLS

Cook Time: 30 minutes

Servings: 6

Ingredients:

- 2 cups cooked chicken, minced
- 1/2 cup oats, ground
- 1/4 cup carrot, grated
- 1/4 cup unsalted chicken broth

Instructions:

1) Mix minced chicken, ground oats, grated carrot, and chicken broth.
2) Form into meatballs and bake until cooked through.

Nutritional Info: Protein: 14g, Fat: 6g, Carbs: 10g

Tips: Use ground oats to help bind the meatballs together.

14) CHICKEN & SPINACH CASSEROLE

Cook Time: 40 minutes

Servings: 5

Ingredients:

- 2 cups cooked chicken, cubed
- 1 cup spinach, chopped
- 1/2 cup pumpkin puree
- 1/4 cup low-sodium chicken broth

Instructions:

1) Mix chicken, chopped spinach, pumpkin puree, and chicken broth in a baking dish.
2) Bake until heated through and serve after cooling.

Nutritional Info: Protein: 22g, Fat: 7g, Carbs: 10g

Tips: Use fresh spinach for maximum nutritional benefits.

15) CHICKEN & ZUCCHINI MASH

Cook Time: 20 minutes

Servings: 3

Ingredients:

- 1 1/2 cups cooked chicken, shredded
- 1 cup zucchini, grated
- 1/4 cup parsley, chopped
- 1 tablespoon coconut oil

Instructions:

1) Mix shredded chicken, grated zucchini, chopped parsley, and coconut oil.
2) Serve once cooled.

Nutritional Info: Protein: 16g, Fat: 6g, Carbs: 8g

Tips: Use a light hand on coconut oil for dogs prone to pancreatitis.

16) CHICKEN & BARLEY STEW

Cook Time: 35 minutes

Servings: 4

Ingredients:

- 2 cups cooked chicken, diced
- 1 cup cooked barley
- 1/2 cup carrots, sliced
- 1/4 cup green beans, chopped

Instructions:

1) Combine diced chicken, cooked barley, sliced carrots, and chopped green beans in a pot.
2) Simmer until vegetables are tender, then serve.

Nutritional Info: Protein: 19g, Fat: 7g, Carbs: 20g

Tips: Opt for whole grain barley for added fiber.

17) CHICKEN & BLUEBERRY BLISS

Cook Time: 20 minutes

Servings: 3

Ingredients:

- 1 cup cooked chicken, chopped
- 1/2 cup blueberries
- 1/4 cup pumpkin puree
- 1 tablespoon olive oil

Instructions:

1) Mix chopped chicken, blueberries, pumpkin puree, and olive oil in a bowl.
2) Serve in appropriate portions for your dog.

Nutritional Info: Protein: 14g, Fat: 5g, Carbs: 8g

Tips: Use unsweetened pumpkin puree for this recipe.

18) CHICKEN & GREEN MIX-UP

Cook Time: 15 minutes

Servings: 2

Ingredients:

- 1 cup cooked chicken, diced
- 1/2 cup green peas
- 1/2 cup green beans, chopped
- 1/4 cup unsalted chicken broth

Instructions:

1) Mix diced chicken, green peas, chopped green beans, and chicken broth in a bowl.
2) Serve in appropriate portions once cooled.

Nutritional Info: Protein: 15g, Fat: 6g, Carbs: 8g

Tips: Use fresh or frozen vegetables for optimal nutrients.

19) CHICKEN & SWEET POTATO HASH

Cook Time: 25 minutes

Servings: 4

Ingredients:

- 2 cups cooked chicken, shredded
- 1 cup sweet potato, cubed
- 1/2 cup kale, finely chopped
- 1 tablespoon coconut oil

Instructions:

1) Sauté sweet potato cubes in coconut oil until tender.
2) Add shredded chicken and chopped kale, cook until heated through.
3) Serve once cooled.

Nutritional Info: Protein: 18g, Fat: 7g, Carbs: 15g

Tips: Kale provides vitamins, but limit the quantity as it can be tough to digest in large amounts.

20) CHICKEN & PEAR SALAD

Cook Time: 15 minutes

Servings: 3

Ingredients:

- 1 1/2 cups cooked chicken, diced
- 1 pear, diced
- 1/4 cup celery, chopped
- 2 tablespoons plain yogurt

Instructions:

1) Mix diced chicken, diced pear, chopped celery, and plain yogurt in a bowl.
2) Serve immediately.

Nutritional Info: Protein: 16g, Fat: 6g, Carbs: 10g

Tips: Remove seeds and core from the pear before dicing.

21) CHICKEN & CARROT SOUFFLÉ

Cook Time: 35 minutes

Servings: 4

Ingredients:

- 2 cups cooked chicken, chopped
- 1 cup carrots, grated
- 1/2 cup low-sodium chicken broth
- 2 eggs

Instructions:

1) Blend chopped chicken, grated carrots, chicken broth, and eggs.
2) Pour into greased ramekins and bake until set.

Nutritional Info: Protein: 20g, Fat: 8g, Carbs: 12g

Tips: Allow the soufflé to cool before serving to avoid burns.

22) CHICKEN & COTTAGE CHEESE WRAP

Cook Time: 20 minutes

Servings: 2

Ingredients:

- 1 cup cooked chicken, shredded
- 1/2 cup cottage cheese
- 2 whole wheat tortillas
- 1/4 cup baby spinach leaves

Instructions:

1) Spread cottage cheese on tortillas, add shredded chicken and baby spinach.
2) Roll up the tortillas and serve.

Nutritional Info: Protein: 15g, Fat: 5g, Carbs: 20g

Tips: Use small tortillas and cut into smaller pieces for smaller dogs.

23) CHICKEN & APPLE SAUTÉ

Cook Time: 20 minutes

Servings: 3

Ingredients:

- 1 1/2 cups cooked chicken, cubed
- 1 apple, thinly sliced
- 1/4 cup green beans, chopped
- 1 tablespoon olive oil

Instructions:

1) Sauté chicken cubes, apple slices, and chopped green beans in olive oil until tender.
2) Serve once cooled.

Nutritional Info: Protein: 18g, Fat: 7g, Carbs: 12g

Tips: Remove seeds and core from the apple before slicing.

24) CHICKEN & SEAWEED SURPRISE

Cook Time: 20 minutes

Servings: 3

Ingredients:

- 1 cup cooked chicken, shredded
- 1/2 cup cooked seaweed (like nori), chopped
- 1/4 cup carrots, grated
- 1 tablespoon sesame oil

Instructions:

1) Mix shredded chicken, chopped seaweed, grated carrots, and sesame oil.
2) Serve once cooled.

Nutritional Info: Protein: 15g, Fat: 6g, Carbs: 8g

Tips: Seaweed provides minerals and vitamins, but use it in moderation.

CHAPTER 4

CHICKEN-BASED TREATS AND SNACKS

25) CHICKEN POPSICLES

Prep Time: 10 minutes

Freezing Time: 3 hours

Servings: 6

Ingredients:

- 1 cup cooked chicken, shredded
- 1/2 cup low-sodium chicken broth

Instructions:

1) Mix shredded chicken and chicken broth.
2) Pour into ice cube trays and freeze.

Nutritional Info: Protein: 10g, Fat: 3g, Carbs: 1g

Tips: Add small dog treats to each cube for an extra surprise.

26) CHICKEN APPLE BITES

Prep Time: 15 minutes

Cook Time: 20 minutes

Servings: 4

Ingredients:

- 1 cup cooked chicken, finely chopped
- 1 apple, peeled and grated
- 1 egg

Instructions:

1) Preheat oven to 350°F (175°C).
2) Mix chopped chicken, grated apple, and egg.
3) Form into small balls and bake until golden brown.

Nutritional Info: Protein: 15g, Fat: 5g, Carbs: 10g

Tips: Use unsweetened apples for a healthier option.

27) CHICKEN CARROT CHEWIES

Prep Time: 15 minutes

Cook Time: 25 minutes

Servings: 8

Ingredients:

- 1 1/2 cups cooked chicken, minced
- 1/2 cup carrots, finely grated
- 1/4 cup oat flour

Instructions:

1) Preheat oven to 325°F (160°C).
2) Mix minced chicken, grated carrots, and oat flour.
3) Shape into sticks and bake until firm.

Nutritional Info: Protein: 18g, Fat: 7g, Carbs: 10g

Tips: Add a touch of honey for extra flavor (optional).

28) CHICKEN CRUNCH WRAPS

Prep Time: 15 minutes

Cook Time: 10 minutes

Servings: 6

Ingredients:

- 1 cup cooked chicken, shredded
- 1/2 cup plain Greek yogurt
- 1/4 cup spinach, finely chopped
- 3 whole wheat tortillas

Instructions:

1) Mix shredded chicken, Greek yogurt, and chopped spinach.
2) Spread onto tortillas, roll up, and cut into smaller pieces.

Nutritional Info: Protein: 12g, Fat: 4g, Carbs: 15g

Tips: Opt for small tortillas for smaller dog breeds.

29) CHICKEN BLUEBERRY BISCUITS

Prep Time: 20 minutes

Cook Time: 30 minutes

Servings: 10

Ingredients:

- 2 cups cooked chicken, minced
- 1/2 cup blueberries
- 1 cup oat flour

Instructions:

1) Preheat oven to 350°F (175°C).
2) Mix minced chicken, blueberries, and oat flour.
3) Form into biscuits and bake until crispy.

Nutritional Info: Protein: 20g, Fat: 8g, Carbs: 15g

Tips: Freeze some biscuits for longer shelf life.

30) CHICKEN SWEET POTATO STRIPS

Prep Time: 10 minutes

Cook Time: 25 minutes

Servings: 4

Ingredients:

- 1 1/2 cups cooked chicken, thinly sliced
- 1 sweet potato, peeled and cut into strips
- 1 tablespoon coconut oil

Instructions:

1) Preheat oven to 375°F (190°C).
2) Toss sweet potato strips in coconut oil, then bake until crisp.
3) Wrap chicken slices around cooled sweet potato strips.

Nutritional Info: Protein: 16g, Fat: 6g, Carbs: 12g

Tips: Use a dehydrator for a chewier texture.

31) CHICKEN & PUMPKIN PUPSICLES

Prep Time: 15 minutes

Freezing Time: 4 hours

Servings: 6

Ingredients:

- 1 cup cooked chicken, diced
- 1/2 cup pumpkin puree
- 1/4 cup plain yogurt

Instructions:

1) Blend diced chicken, pumpkin puree, and yogurt until smooth.
2) Pour into ice cube trays and freeze.

Nutritional Info: Protein: 12g, Fat: 5g, Carbs: 8g

Tips: Add a pinch of cinnamon for extra flavor.

32) CHICKEN & CRANBERRY BITES

Prep Time: 15 minutes

Cook Time: 20 minutes

Servings: 5

Ingredients:

- 1 1/2 cups cooked chicken, chopped
- 1/4 cup cranberries, finely chopped
- 1/2 cup almond flour

Instructions:

1) Preheat oven to 350°F (175°C).
2) Mix chopped chicken, chopped cranberries, and almond flour.
3) Form into bite-sized balls and bake until cooked through.

Nutritional Info: Protein: 14g, Fat: 6g, Carbs: 10g

Tips: Use unsweetened cranberries for a healthier option.

33) CHICKEN ZUCCHINI CHIPS

Prep Time: 15 minutes

Cook Time: 30 minutes

Servings: 4

Ingredients:

- 1 cup cooked chicken, shredded
- 1 zucchini, thinly sliced
- 1 tablespoon olive oil

Instructions:

1) Preheat oven to 225°F (110°C).
2) Toss zucchini slices in olive oil, then bake until crispy.
3) Top each slice with shredded chicken.

Nutritional Info: Protein: 14g, Fat: 6g, Carbs: 8g

Tips: Use a mandolin for uniform zucchini slices.

34) CHICKEN SPINACH MEATBALLS

Prep Time: 20 minutes

Cook Time: 25 minutes

Servings: 6

Ingredients:

- 1 1/2 cups cooked chicken, minced
- 1/2 cup spinach, finely chopped
- 1/4 cup quinoa, cooked

Instructions:

1) Preheat oven to 375°F (190°C).
2) Mix minced chicken, chopped spinach, and cooked quinoa.
3) Form into small meatballs and bake until cooked through.

Nutritional Info: Protein: 18g, Fat: 7g, Carbs: 12g

Tips: Steam spinach to make it easier to digest for dogs.

35) CHICKEN & CHEESE CHEWSTICKS

Prep Time: 15 minutes

Cook Time: 30 minutes

Servings: 8

Ingredients:

- 1 1/2 cups cooked chicken, shredded
- 1/2 cup shredded cheese
- 1/4 cup oat flour

Instructions:

1) Preheat oven to 350°F (175°C).
2) Mix shredded chicken, shredded cheese, and oat flour.
3) Shape into sticks and bake until firm.

Nutritional Info: Protein: 20g, Fat: 9g, Carbs: 10g

Tips: Use low-fat cheese for a healthier option.

36) CHICKEN & CARROT POPS

Prep Time: 15 minutes

Freezing Time: 4 hours

Servings: 6

Ingredients:

- 1 cup cooked chicken, finely chopped
- 1/2 cup carrot, grated
- 1/4 cup chicken broth

Instructions:

1) Mix chopped chicken, grated carrot, and chicken broth.
2) Pour into ice cube trays and freeze.

Nutritional Info: Protein: 14g, Fat: 5g, Carbs: 8g

Tips: Use silicone molds for easier removal.

37) CHICKEN & PUMPKIN BISCUITS

Prep Time: 20 minutes

Cook Time: 25 minutes

Servings: 12

Ingredients:

- 2 cups cooked chicken, minced
- 1/2 cup pumpkin puree
- 1 1/4 cups oat flour

Instructions:

1) Preheat oven to 350°F (175°C).
2) Mix minced chicken, pumpkin puree, and oat flour.
3) Form into biscuits and bake until golden brown.

Nutritional Info: Protein: 22g, Fat: 8g, Carbs: 15g

Tips: Use pumpkin without added sugars or spices.

38) CHICKEN & SPINACH PUPCAKES

Prep Time: 20 minutes

Cook Time: 30 minutes

Servings: 8

Ingredients:

- 2 cups cooked chicken, shredded
- 1/2 cup spinach, finely chopped
- 1/4 cup unsweetened applesauce

Instructions:

1) Preheat oven to 350°F (175°C).
2) Mix shredded chicken, chopped spinach, and applesauce.
3) Spoon into cupcake molds and bake until set.

Nutritional Info: Protein: 24g, Fat: 10g, Carbs: 15g

Tips: Use silicone molds for easy removal.

39) CHICKEN & CARROT COOKIES

Prep Time: 15 minutes

Cook Time: 25 minutes

Servings: 10

Ingredients:

- 1 1/2 cups cooked chicken, minced
- 1/2 cup grated carrots
- 1/4 cup coconut flour

Instructions:

1) Preheat oven to 350°F (175°C).
2) Mix minced chicken, grated carrots, and coconut flour.
3) Form into cookie shapes and bake until firm.

Nutritional Info: Protein: 18g, Fat: 7g, Carbs: 10g

Tips: Store in an airtight container for freshness.

40) CHICKEN & PARSLEY BONES

Prep Time: 20 minutes

Cook Time: 30 minutes

Servings: 8

Ingredients:

- 2 cups cooked chicken, finely chopped
- 1/2 cup fresh parsley, chopped
- 1/4 cup brown rice flour

Instructions:

1) Preheat oven to 350°F (175°C).

2) Mix chopped chicken, chopped parsley, and brown rice flour.

3) Shape into bone-like figures and bake until crispy.

Nutritional Info: Protein: 22g, Fat: 8g, Carbs: 12g

Tips: Use cookie cutters for fun shapes.

41) CHICKEN & GREEN BEAN CRUNCHIES

Prep Time: 15 minutes

Cook Time: 20 minutes

Servings: 6

Ingredients:

- 1 1/2 cups cooked chicken, shredded
- 1/2 cup green beans, finely chopped
- 1/4 cup chickpea flour

Instructions:

1) Preheat oven to 350°F (175°C).
2) Mix shredded chicken, chopped green beans, and chickpea flour.
3) Form into small discs and bake until crunchy.

Nutritional Info: Protein: 20g, Fat: 7g, Carbs: 10g

Tips: Use fresh green beans for optimal flavor.

42) CHICKEN & OAT BARS

Prep Time: 20 minutes

Cook Time: 30 minutes

Servings: 10

Ingredients:

- 2 cups cooked chicken, minced
- 1/2 cup oats
- 1/4 cup honey (optional)

Instructions:

1) Preheat oven to 350°F (175°C).
2) Mix minced chicken, oats, and honey (if using).
3) Press into a baking dish and bake until set.

Nutritional Info: Protein: 24g, Fat: 10g, Carbs: 15g

Tips: Use unsweetened oats for a healthier option.

CHAPTER 5
FAQs AND TROUBLESHOOTING

COMMON CONCERNS ABOUT CHICKEN-BASED DIETS

As you embark on the journey of crafting homemade chicken-based meals for your canine companion, it's natural to encounter certain concerns or doubts. Let's address these to ensure you're well-equipped to provide the best for your furry friend.

Is Chicken Safe for Dogs?

Absolutely! Chicken is a fantastic protein source for dogs, offering essential amino acids crucial for their growth and overall health. However, it's essential to serve it cooked thoroughly, avoiding bones and seasoned preparations. Also, ensure you've removed excess fat and skin, as they might not sit well with your dog's digestive system.

Should I Worry About Allergies to Chicken?

While food allergies in dogs are possible, they are relatively rare. Chicken allergies, specifically, are not as common as some other allergens. However, if your dog displays symptoms like itching, skin issues, or digestive distress after consuming chicken, consult your vet for guidance. Remember, every dog's system is unique.

Can I Feed Only Chicken to My Dog?

Variety is key! While chicken is a great protein source, a balanced diet for your dog should include a mix of proteins, vegetables, and grains. Feeding only chicken may lead to nutritional deficiencies. Rotate chicken with other proteins like beef, turkey, or fish, and incorporate a range of dog-friendly veggies and carbs.

ADDRESSING DIGESTIVE ISSUES

When transitioning to homemade chicken-based meals, digestive issues can sometimes arise. Here's how to navigate and troubleshoot them:

Diarrhea or Upset Stomach

It's not uncommon for dogs to experience digestive upset when transitioning to new foods. If your dog experiences diarrhea or an upset stomach, consider slowing down the transition. Gradually introduce the homemade meals by mixing them with their regular food over a week or more. This gradual shift allows their system to adjust.

Food Intolerances or Allergies

If your dog displays symptoms of an allergy or food intolerance (like itching, vomiting, or diarrhea), it might indicate sensitivity to an ingredient in the recipe. Review the ingredients, and if necessary, consult with your vet to identify the allergen.

Portion Control and Overfeeding

Feeding too much can lead to digestive discomfort. Ensure you're following portion guidelines according to your dog's weight and activity level. Overfeeding can cause indigestion or weight issues. Use measuring tools to maintain accuracy.

TRANSITIONING YOUR DOG TO HOMEMADE FOOD

Transitioning your dog from commercial to homemade food requires patience and a gradual shift. Here's a step-by-step guide to ensure a smooth transition:

Consult Your Veterinarian

Before transitioning, consult your vet. They can offer guidance based on your dog's specific needs, including the right portion sizes, nutrient requirements, and potential health considerations.

Gradual Transition

Start by replacing a small portion of your dog's regular food with the homemade meal. Over the course of a week or more, gradually increase the proportion of homemade food while decreasing the commercial food. Monitor for any digestive issues during this transition period.

Observation and Adjustments

Watch for any changes in your dog's behavior, stool, or overall health during the transition. If there are concerns or digestive issues, slow down the transition process or adjust ingredients to suit your dog's needs.

Balanced Diet

Ensure the homemade meals provide a balanced diet, including proteins, carbohydrates, healthy fats, and essential vitamins and minerals. Variety is essential, so aim for a mix of ingredients to cover all nutritional requirements.

Consistency and Patience

Consistency is key in the transition process. Stick to a routine and be patient. Your dog might take time to adjust to new flavors and textures, but with time, they'll likely come to enjoy their homemade meals.

Transitioning your dog to homemade food can be a rewarding experience, offering them nutritious and wholesome meals tailored to their specific needs.

CONCLUSION

As I pen down these final words, my heart swells with an overwhelming sense of gratitude, love, and a deep connection fostered through our shared passion for our furry friends. To each and every dog lover who has walked alongside me through the pages of this book, I extend my sincerest thanks— a thanks that transcends mere words and delves into the depths of heartfelt appreciation.

This journey, this collaborative effort in exploring the world of homemade chicken-based dog food, has been nothing short of transformative. It's been a journey woven with the threads of devotion, empathy, and a relentless pursuit of providing the very best for our beloved pets. And as we conclude this chapter, I want to express the profound impact your commitment has made on me, on the lives of countless dogs, and on the future of canine nutrition.

The bond we share with our dogs transcends the realms of mere companionship; it's a sacred connection steeped in unconditional love and unwavering loyalty. And it's this very bond that fuels our quest to ensure their well-being, to craft meals that not only nourish their bodies but also feed their souls.

Each recipe within these pages is more than just a list of ingredients and instructions; it's a testament to the dedication poured into every whisk, every stir, and every carefully measured portion. They are a reflection of our collective commitment to providing our furry companions with meals that surpass mere sustenance, meals that are crafted with love and care.

But this journey doesn't conclude here; rather, it's a stepping stone into a future where homemade, health-conscious dog food becomes a cornerstone of every pet owner's routine. It's a pledge to continue evolving, refining, and expanding our understanding of what constitutes the ideal nutrition for our dogs.

As I bid you adieu for now, I implore you to take these recipes not just as instructions but as invitations to create moments of joy, health, and connection with your canine companions. Let the aroma of simmering chicken and the joy of cooking for your pet become rituals that strengthen the bond you share.

And in the spirit of this shared journey, I invite you to grace me with your feedback, your thoughts, and your stories. Your experiences with these recipes are invaluable—guiding lights that illuminate the path for fellow dog lovers. Your insights will shape the future, ensuring that every dog, no matter where they wag their tail, is met with nourishment, love, and well-deserved happiness.

I extend my deepest gratitude for your unwavering support, your trust, and your dedication to the well-being of our furry friends. May these recipes continue to bring warmth to your kitchen, joy to your dog's bowl, and an abundance of tail wags to your home.

With boundless appreciation and heartfelt thanks

MONTH:_____

SUN	MON	TUE	WED	THU	FRI	SAT

	BREAKFAST	LUNCH	DINNER
MEALS TO TRY			

MONTH:_____

SUN	MON	TUE	WED	THU	FRI	SAT

	BREAKFAST	LUNCH	DINNER
MEALS TO TRY			

MONTH:_____

SUN	MON	TUE	WED	THU	FRI	SAT

	BREAKFAST	LUNCH	DINNER
MEALS TO TRY			

MONTH:_____

SUN	MON	TUE	WED	THU	FRI	SAT

	BREAKFAST	LUNCH	DINNER
MEALS TO TRY			

MONTH:_____

SUN	MON	TUE	WED	THU	FRI	SAT

	BREAKFAST	LUNCH	DINNER
MEALS TO TRY			

CHICKEN BASED DOG FOOD COOKBOOK

MONTH:_____

SUN	MON	TUE	WED	THU	FRI	SAT

	BREAKFAST	LUNCH	DINNER
MEALS TO TRY			

MONTH:_____

SUN	MON	TUE	WED	THU	FRI	SAT

	BREAKFAST	LUNCH	DINNER
MEALS TO TRY			

MONTH: _____

SUN	MON	TUE	WED	THU	FRI	SAT

	BREAKFAST	LUNCH	DINNER
MEALS TO TRY			

MONTH:_____

SUN	MON	TUE	WED	THU	FRI	SAT

	BREAKFAST	LUNCH	DINNER
MEALS TO TRY			

MONTH: _____

SUN	MON	TUE	WED	THU	FRI	SAT

	BREAKFAST	LUNCH	DINNER
MEALS TO TRY			

MONTH:_____

SUN	MON	TUE	WED	THU	FRI	SAT

	BREAKFAST	LUNCH	DINNER
MEALS TO TRY			

CHICKEN BASED DOG FOOD COOKBOOK

MONTH:_____

SUN	MON	TUE	WED	THU	FRI	SAT

	BREAKFAST	LUNCH	DINNER
MEALS TO TRY			

Made in United States
Troutdale, OR
02/23/2024

17937236R00046